For Paul Vaughan

Acknowledgements

The following poems have previously been published elsewhere, sometimes in earlier forms:

Fall and *Definitions of a Shipwreck* in *Algebra of Owls*, *Taxonomy* in *Poetry on Spiders* (Fair Acre Press, 2015), *Why a Southern Jessie is drawn to the Yorkshire Dales* in *Bee's Breakfast* (Beautiful Dragons, 2017), *First Climb* in *100,000 poets for Change* (2017), *Eclipse* and *Lost in the Wood* in *More Exhibitionism* (Stairwell Books, 2016), *The Angler* in *Dreamcatcher*, *Discalced* in *Perfect Timing* (Createspace, 2014).

Also by Hannah Stone:

Lodestone, Stairwell Books, 2016.

Contributions to *An After-Dinner's Sleep* (with Gill Lambert and Maria Preston), Indigo Dreams Publishing, 2015.

New Crops from Old Fields: Eight Medievalist Poets, ed. Oz Hardwick, Stairwell Books, 2015.

CONTENTS

Missing Miles

Fall

First snow. Less hyperbolic than forecast.
So it may be with fall out;
the punters get things wrong.
The daily pattern continues. People rise,
get washed and dress, and break their fasts
whatever latitude they inhabit.
In this neck of the woods
the sun did not deign to show itself,
but I answered emails, fed cats.
Conversations with tongues and thumbs
brought no solace.
As daylight seeped back over the horizon
a bowl of apples needed peeling,
and whatsoever bits of them were lovely,
and of any virtue,
I sliced and cooked.
We will still eat, and sleep,
and wake to find the nightmare still around,
and search again, tomorrow,
for whatsoever things are true
or just or pure or of good report,
and keep on looking.
And don't expect divine intervention
to make a difference. It's our job
to find the tools or make new ones.
Man is the animal that does this.

Missing miles

'FP Castle Bolton, 2 ½ miles.'
The gate swings open,
brushing nettles and benign cow parsley,
leading to a path curving perversely
through rough sweet stubble,
yielding to the sudden cool of a thicket
of alders and willows, muddy boot prints
beside a plank bridge.
Then, uncut hay sighs as you pass through it,
looking for the next finger post.

'FP Castle Bolton, 2 ½ miles.'
The charitable view might be
that the surveyor got distracted
by the curlew cranking open
his scimitar beak to split
the still air, or lost concentration
when a stone barn appeared, filling
the summer sky with fidgets of swallows.

Maybe it was a light-fingered cartographer,
hungry for a taste of summer peace.
He hears the essence of the landscape
in the peewit's peevish cry,
gets the measure of the drystone walls,
gathers the aimless sheep
and a handful of meadow crane-bill
and folds the missing half mile into his pocket.

Why a Southern Jessie is Drawn to the Yorkshire Dales

Sudden snow redrafts this landscape.
Overnight, the sanctuary of stone walls
becomes an ovine mortuary.
For an instant, the hills take the same device
that millennia used to engrave catscradles of valleys
onto the Askrigg Block; ice
teasing troughs and peaks from grit and limestone;
thaw-water pressing punctures into slabs,
breaking them into rocks men pile round pastures,
hunch up as hay barns.
And, come the spring, orphaned bones
in the windward lee of walls sink
below fresh grass, and lambs
headbutt quick currents of air,
stage acrobatic stunts on maternal backs,
heedless of market day and Sunday roasts.
Calloused hands heft into place
chunks of stone no mortice holds in place.
Judgment secures them. It's in the genes,
with the wordless piping that steers
the sheepdog to chivvy the ewes.
I'm drawn by this, not ossified.
My urban soul is laved by peaty waterfalls;
drystone walls are the jesses which save me craving
the strange foods of my southern youth.
These days, I hunt with the wind.

Taxonomy

From the summit I saw them placing red flags,
like players on the roughest of crazy golf courses,
but this is Buckden Pike, not Scarborough.
Halfway down, sinewy tubs and tubes came into focus.
The men's gesticulations acquired gravitas,
Their signals now became forensic.

What were they looking for, I asked?
Semljicola Caliginosus, a spider so shy
she hadn't been logged since 2013.
The arachnologist tickled its name
onto my hand with his pen,
so I could google it, when reception returned.

Nearing Starbotton, I reached
to stroke fresh bracken fronds
that nudged their knuckles
through last year's growth;
one of the eight legs washed
off onto their damp green curls.

Next to go was her *clypeus*, 'what passes for a face,'
rinsed into a stream with a smear of sheepshit.
My fingers grazed a stile, and the wet wood
caught the sensory hairs
about whose function
entomologists speculate in furious uncertainty.

By the time I'd reached the village,
where I parted from the scientists,
every feeler and leg of the rare *linyphiidae*,
and all of her bashful functions
had secreted themselves once more
beneath cushions of sphagnum moss.

Territorial dispute

Aesthetically, I admit I am charmed
by the casual symmetry
of stripes, the voluptuous
moist opening into which you retreat
but, snail, this is contested land.

This is mine, my more than space and time
hedged between the strident calls
of kitchen and office,
boundaried by marking and ironing,

my space for welcoming the fall
of freckled sunlight wriggling
through unpruned boughs,
for relishing the quickening
of green spears knifing their way
through recalcitrant soil,
for blessing the gracious fruit
which colours as it swells,

my time for tranquil minutes
after breakfast, culling handfuls
of rocket and parsley
to sharpen my mid-day salad,
for popping out at dusk to gather laundry
which has spent my absence
absorbing the garden's fragrance.
and the occasional spider.

I've been kind and patient, all day –
now, it's war with molluscs –
death by the blue pellet,
or the rank sweetness
of the beer trap.

Morning Service

I still believe in birdsong.
This morning, in place of the weekday clamour
of the stadium, church bells cascade
their appeal to the faithful.

On my plot, I settle
to serious digging. I hear the robin
before I find him, perched
amidst unharvested apples.

I pause to stretch, and search
for my pastor. His throat quivers
as the small hinge of his beak opens
and his call falls through damp air.

After the hymns of praise, he delivers a homily
about worms, and I listen as I tear apart
the white metastasis of bindweed,
unthreading tendrils from the tines.

He has my ear, persuades me
to share his vision
for this new Eden. I am penitent
about the paucity of worms.

Winter Solstice

The shops are crammed
with sugared-up kids
badgering list-toting parents,

and the seasonal staff
in sweaty Christmas jumpers
smile, and count their zero hours.

Empty-handed, I walk
the long way home
beside the stream in the woods.

Dogs are taking their owners
for an afternoon constitutional,
and there is nothing to stop for,

but beech trees liming
the last of the light,
and, on dogwood and empty elder,

robins hanging one bead of song
after another
on a muslin sky.

First Climb

At night the bees are sleepy
and not suspicious.
This will be spiritual food,
so when the harvesters have gathered
(eight or nine of them to circle the tree)
we share the words of the prayer.

O Mother Bee,
let me harvest your honey,
to give to my children

we chant, but softly,
so the bees slumber on.
Bare feet crackle on twigs
as more men arrive.

The old hands go first,
nodding towards footholds,
pointing out crevices in the bark
that will span the ninety feet ascent.

Young men like me with pounding hearts
rub soft palms together, and stretch up
towards the dark sky. I try
to forget the night-curdling blast
of sound as my father fell, years ago,
splintering branches then his spine.

For his sake I climb tonight,
my prize not honey but approbation.
Up, up, up, no light, nothing breaks
the silence but the laboured breathing
of the climbers. The tree quivers
as we reach our goal. So this is it.

Now I must twist, and drop
upside down, to reach the nest.

Fear has no place here, it unmans
this sacred calling. If you fall,
the whole village will catch you,
and nurse your brokenness
till death reknits your shattered self.

I loosen one hand, then the other.
It is time to let go.

Eclipse

Sky opaque as Tupperware is standard
in Central London; eighty five percent
of sunlight blocked from southeast England
fails to cast apocalyptic gloom

on suited men, who beetle underground
en route to mining the nation's wealth,
while street sleepers slither from sleeping bags,
modern mendicants with Starbucks begging bowls.

It's not darkness, but the sudden chill
that drills into your consciousness
as mercury shows a three degree drop
and for a few moments exhaled breath spirals

in white bursts round buds breaking
on peeling plane trees. Tell it to the bees?
Maybe, but it's bones that register
the last ice age, sense the one to come.

Lost in the Wood

'Come-bye, Jack!' A call startles the silence.
My feet, negotiating latticed tree roots, falter;
flurrying thoughts pause.

On the ridge across the gully
a striding silhouette works his collie;
scurrying white shapes are stubborn sheep.

The path twists round; streams emerge
from their limestone cache and chatter to me;
the shepherd's left behind.

I envy his sheep.

Summoning a commanding voice, I project
the instruction to my wayward brain –
'Away! Away to me! Stand!'
'Lie Down.'

Dumb Phone

You took me for dinner at your club.
There was crisp linen, bright lights,
and sharp menus. Some of the wines
cost more than an entire meal.

You placed a brace of smart-phones
on the table between us,
and leaned across them,
so you could take my hand in yours.

The waiter poured wine into sparking glasses,
then moved the bottle to a separate table
so the perfume you'd bought me
wouldn't taint its aroma.

We ate, in silence. From time to time,
the Blackberries winked at each other.
I looked across the table,
but I couldn't catch your eye.

LinkedIn

Our first anniversary,
you placed diamonds on my unsuspecting finger,
causing a chemical reaction; by the next equinox,
those sparky carbon chips had iced you up.
Now an electronic portal updates me with your skills;
'Risk Management' – important stuff!
The profile pic is still passport approved;
the psychopathic gaze above locked-in lips,
a face slipped on over the fresh-shaved cheek
that rested, once, on my breast at dawn,
entrusting an image of yourself
for safekeeping in my sleepy eyes,
neglecting as you sprinted for the 6.15
to pocket the silken thread I'd spun
to guide you safely home from an amazed city.

Penelope

It ended up a dry season,
full of quiet desperation.
I was drawing with a leaky bucket
from an almost empty well,

my words trickling over the surface
of unbroken soil; ground
too compacted
for anything to root or thrive.

Fears curdled our conversation
into silences neither companionable
nor peaceful, but peopled
with constraints, fractions

of reasons, procrastination,
bafflement. So you retreated
into an arid labyrinth, and, stich by stich,
each night, I unpicked hope's tapestry.

This Folder is Empty

Control plus 'H' sorts the browsing history.
You've deleted the emails,
and confused vapour-trails of 'sent' messages.
Departure is imminent.

All you can sense is the rising pitch of jets
before abandonment screeches into the air
in a bumpy take off, and you swallow hard:
see how the solid ground vanishes

as your ears fill with white sound.
Then you float between the bright sky
and storm clouds, one finger tracing the icon
of this plane, tracking to an unknown destination.

You scroll down the address list,
and press a button or two: something's gone.
'This folder is empty'
is the message under the cursor.

The pressure builds, as the descent begins.
Landing smoothly, seatbelt discarded,
Lord, you beg,
erase him from my hard drive.

Definitions of a Shipwreck

5pm – unusual time for him to text.
Just seen a professional. Confirms I have serious issues.
Too drained to talk tonight, if you don't mind.
I was patient, tried not to hassle him.
Twisted the 'commitment' ring he'd placed
on my third finger three months before
to *remind you what you mean to me.*

Channels of communication closed, one by one.
The telephone seemed out of bounds, at least
until he'd *got his head into a better place.*
My pulse raced when his name pinged
into my inbox, but there was little enough to read.
Eventually, I got the drift.

Jetsam: part of a ship, its equipment, or its cargo, that is purposely cast overboard or jettisoned to lighten the load in times of distress, and is washed ashore.

A turbulent time followed, fear
mostly flooding hope, though both
bobbed up and down on the waves.
I clutched at straws. Finally, he roused himself,
spelled it out blatantly.

Lagan: goods or wreckage that is lying on the bottom of the ocean, sometimes marked by a buoy, which can be reclaimed.

I offered alternatives, compromise.
A patch of grass beside the bench is seared
into my memory, marking where I sat
when I last heard his voice.
I asked about the ring, which I'd swapped
from left hand to right. Silence
was eloquence, or was the signal breaking up?

He posted back my house keys,
bundled the designer dresses
into cardboard cartons
that hi-jacked me at work one morning,
blocking up the post room.

Derelict: cargo that is also on the bottom of the ocean, but which no-one has any hope of reclaiming. May also refer to a drifting, abandoned ship.

The Angler

"The light fly does usually make the most sport in a dark day,
and the darkest and least fly in a bright or clear day."
Izaak Walton, *The Complete Angler*, 1653.

You were a natural, from the start,
lured me with words like 'remarkable',
'a neglected jewel.'
You laid down night hooks in bedtime texts,
signed off 'G, kiss', before close-down.
Then you added enticements, hooked me
on Jo Malone and first class travel.

The bathrooms in our separate homes
acquired mirror image supplies –
your expensive mouthwash, my budget moisturiser.
One weekend you brought with you the last
of your everyday Dunhill cologne
(not the posh one you wore with the 2K watch).
It slopped in a squat bottle,
square and solid as a tiny fishtank,
its thick walls surrounding
a curved pool, where your fragrance
was a peachy puddle.

Left alone, I pick books off the shelves,
skim them for answers. I find that
the trout-fisher should vary his flies
according to the season; in early May
the ruddy fly is best: it has *a body made of red wool,*
wrapt about with black silk.

I still wear the cashmere sweater dress,
pair it with leggings you'd never have allowed,
and sometimes, just for myself, I unwind
a pair of the hold-ups you supplied
as approved hosiery. It's then I find
the dead weight of your weekend scent,
stored in my lingerie drawer.

If I press hard enough, I can release
a whiff of you into my hand,
though you are long gone, and your touch
is distorted in my memory just like my fingers
viewed at blurry angles through the heavy glass.
It seems as if there should be
so much more of you than dregs.
As I roll the stockings up my legs, I feel the tug
of the line you cast, again and again
from strong shoulders, onto the ripples of my desire.

In the autumn, the best lure is
thread of gold or silver, silk of several colours;
especially sad-coloured, to make the fly's head.
I sprayed my cashmere with cedar oil, to deter moths,
wrapped my jewellery in acid-free tissue.
They're preserved unblemished, though unwrapped
I feel the shadow of you, my departed angler,
standing between the sun and the water,
using *a long line and not a little hook.*

Stormy Weather

Marooned with grief, I spin and float toward
that sly tormentor Sleep, who flirts with me
throughout the night: his promises afford
no break from memory's duplicity.
Round midnight, to silence the dialogue
inside my head, I tune the radio
to World Service news. Then, through the fog
of angry pain, new thoughts begin to grow,
though no fresh wind fills the sails before dawn.
Persistence is discarded love's mistake,
casting me adrift, rendering me torn,
exploited, enfeebled, dumb. At day break,
the weather forecaster predicts for me
a new low, losing its identity.

Casting out the Ballast

For Oz Hardwick

Hot air balloons remind you of summer,
you post, beneath an image
of a bold red disc balanced
on bright blue sky.

The days are shorter now; their greyness
compresses me. I miss those afternoons
when you would hold up to the light
threadbare scraps of my first drafts,

see through their pretence, suggest
how I might trim or hem those flat sacs,
patch them into possibilities
for me to breathe into,

like the much-mended paper globes I hang
on the Christmas tree, below the star.
I never did write that poem about shoelaces:
perhaps it's waiting to take me unawares.

Changing Gear

The week after I relinquished
a big, bad wolf of a job,
I started to sift the boxes of papers
that had contained my role,

rationalising long-kept notes
of other people's evidence,
recycling redundant knowledge;
shifting up to the loft things to be kept.

Here, cobwebs are sketchy traps
holding now abandoned prey;
hollowed husks of wasps
scattered in segments on the floor.

The new files find companions
with faded labels,
messages in bottles
from a past now all at sea.

I open the velux window,
watch dust motes whirl
in the influx of cool air;
catch sounds from the outside world,

a bee bumbling
high above flower beds,
next door's grandchildren
planning garden games,

a car changing gear
halfway up the hill,
taking someone to a destination
I do not need to name.

Suburban Daphne

Hot work, cutting the hedge on Sunday afternoon.
Ablutions rinse from her sweaty breast
a leaf or two of laurel.

Suburban Daphne fears metamorphosis
into bourgeois conformity,
hears her doom approaching

in the revving of power-tools, as neighbours
arm themselves to trim lawns, blast clean patios,
and strike the silence into submission.

Apollo jogs past in Reeboks,
beat hissing from headphones,
his pumping arms skimming the hedge.

Leaving her towel slumped on the floor
she takes to her heels,
butt-naked, heading for the woods.

Wet footprints track her flight
from the still dripping shower, while the car
on the driveway stays unwashed.

On Re-reading Ovid's Metamorphoses

They were sex-mad, those crafty gods and goddesses,
but, lacking sixpacks and the right hair-stylists,
relied on low cunning and shape-changing
to get their ends away, or punish
divine spouses for over-earthly desires.

Jupiter had some tricks up his sleeve;
a shower of golden rain
to get Danaë up the spout,
and a white bull's hide to wriggle into
so he could run off with Europa, Agenor's child.

But Semele! We've Juno to thank for that debacle.
Jealous as only an ageing goddess can become,
she borrowed the form of her rival's old nurse,
tricking the star-struck girl into begging
her double-dealing lover for a deathblow:

Enough of this celebrity business.
Let me see you as you really are!

Even his lightest thunderbolt was enough
to blast the poor girl into smithereens,
but, as the lightning sped towards her, he snatched
the bun from her oven,
stitched it to his own thigh till it was done.

Twice-born Bacchus spent the rest of his natural
boozing and belching,
and in the hereafter, was pressed into service,
posing with bunches of grapes
for painters keen to make a bob or two.

You can catch his devotee today;
he'll be propping up the bar
after a session in the gym,
branded tee shirt sculpting honed abs,
a regular Adonis in Adidas.

Hubris

Blink, and you'd miss him,
Brueghel's Icarus – such an incidental
to the pastoral scene,
his final moments shot through
with contrasting sensations,

the melting wax scorching his shoulders,
then congealing like blood,
and the salt chill rushing upwards;
the world upended in an instant,
vertical about to flatline.

On a different plane
there is a small space
between ambition and hubris,
the missable instant
just before the plan
starts unravelling,

and there's barely time
to draw breath, before
falling through the hole
in the fabric of intention,
heading for dark matter.

Trading Insults

Old Coppernose, Lion of Justice, Ploughpenny,
Priesthater, Longshanks, He of the Little Dagger –
some cognomens are worth the barter, but even a monarch
cannot choose his legacy. By comparison,
today's abuse seems stripped and crude;
Wanker! We shout at the driver who cuts us up,
Knobhead! Tosser! Cunt!

Gender discourse is all the rage;
we bandy sexual putdowns,
so we remember you, Softsword,
when we see coy adverts for Viagra,
or during tactful moments in bed
when so much is best left unsaid.

Unmanly, too, your other sobriquet,
for what's a man without his land?
You no doubt blamed the barons, or the Pope
other men, wielding their signifiers of fame,
replicating their power in golden shafts
and semiotic jewelled spheres.

Technically, you weren't a bastard,
John Lackland, but, none the less,
I harden my heart
against the illegitimacy
of a man so ready to exploit,
so very quick to turn away.

Seasonal Meeting of the Cousins

Babushka turns her back
on the holy family;
unblinking stares at the radiator.
It's not for her, this baby in a manger business.
But look, says the infant inside her,
there are camels, almost as tall as the shepherds,
and you don't get those in Vladivostok.
Please can we join the queue?
Why should those men have all the fun
(even if they do have presents carved into their mitts)?

So the bright, bulbous kernel
of the doll is unpacked,
joins the menagerie
and gazes with shiny dilated pupils
at the cruciform chunk of olive tree
stretched out on a coffin lid
beneath a watchful wooden mother
and a cuckolded father.
Camel boy wishes, not for the first time,
his charges didn't spit so much.

Play Time

It speaks to her of disembowelment,
that pulling of snapped laces;
thin guts screaming their way through apertures,
then lying piled on the floor beside splayed skins
of unfastened leather uppers.

Oh, how she stretches and twists,
silent in the primal chase,
nicking the tugged taunt with a claw,
taut mouth jerking along its slippery length.

Parking her dignity on the sofa,
she leaps up, then backwards arches.
How wide and cold her yellow eyes!
Feral greed swallows her friendly purr.

And in the morning on the stairs,
the gift is frayed, abandoned.
She walks on velvet now it's time
for hands to yank open a tin of meat.

Liminalities

For Adam

Green sheet demarcates
the space for two lifesavers
to work, each facing the other.

At one end, a chaplain prepares
an infant soul for eternity,
blessed oils anointing

skin so thin
it barely separates
unripe organs from sterile world.

Beyond the protecting veil
the surgeon's tools are sharper,
her hands enacting

the science of prayer
in the rethreading
of a catheter.

Please See the Website for Details of our Helpline

For Jenny Hill

She saw dust rising from the rubble,
tears streaking down cheeks.
She smelled escaped gas,
the ruptured sewer.
She heard screams, sirens
heavy lifting equipment.
She adjusted the earpiece
so the signal was optimal.

She spoke of the international response,
of a wall that had fallen,
exposing a dining room expecting
a family gathering, not this.
She spoke of the fine glass vase
that trembled, unshattered, on the table.

She went home.
The door had all its hinges in place.
She poured hot water
onto coffee grounds.
She observed that as she pushed the plunger
her hand started to shake,
and her ribcage writhed,
and her throat spasmed with dry sobs.
She noticed her cheeks were wet,
and later she sat very still.

A64

Diggers accessing the building site
halt pre-dawn traffic. Commuting drivers
tap steering wheels in time with their stereos,
counterpointing the JCB's manoeuvres.

Es ist vollbracht, sings an alto, with conviction.
But nothing is finished on this stretch of road,
where all day long, while I'm planted at my desk,
trucks choreograph another groundhog day.

Retracing the miles as night falls
I watch the same firefly ballet of headlights
penetrating the dusk with dancing beams
as they pitch over uneven ground.

Left and right, they rehearse their moves,
up and down, like the gear lever
under my palm, which mimics this line-dance.
Sighing, I drive on before the cadence.

Marie Therèse

Observing my slightly reddened eyes
a colleague asks: *Are you okay?*
Oh yes, I'm fine, I prevaricate, walk on,
passing off my affliction as a minor bereavement
or domestic spat. The fact is, simply,
that I accompanied my commute to work
with the last twenty minutes of *Der Rosenkavalier*.

Words alone cannot express this experience:
my mind can frame the nuances of orchestration,
supply a list of musical techniques.
Hearing distils the essence of it all;
the artful pacing, yoking of voices,
but reason cannot explain the effect.

It's opera, so of course the plot is silly,
but, remembering the touch of a lover, I suspect
that a composer who can sustain
such soaring heights of yearning,
climb these peaks of feeling,
might be pretty good in bed.

Discalced

He's fine, your carer says,
he's lost a shoe but seems happy going barefoot.
I thank her and return to my meeting
distracted by the thought of you
steadying one foot at a time
on the fifteen treads of the stairs,
your toes leaning into the deep pile
as you go up then down because
you don't remember why up
or even what 'up' is.

And I try to take an interest
in a smart spreadsheet,
pleased to think you'll be wearing socks
in a nice shade of fawn
(the colour of post-war frugality)
and that she made these for you,
fingers flashing the four silver spears
which clacked and chattered as she turned the heel
knitting her love into each pair,
something you can run your fingers over
because, now that words are treacherous,
textures console.

And I plan to make for your birthday
a patchwork cushion from scraps
of warm Welsh wool, edged with blanket stitch,
and I'll show your hands its narrative
of elusive shades from a forgotten land.
Suddenly this seems so much more urgent
than commenting on the coded cells
which populate the page – a necessary ministry,
a laying on of hands.

Serving Suggestion

At lunchtime,
I pick up the menu of betrayal
and select some explanations.

As starters, some fumblings
about exhausted options,
burn-out, respite care.

For the main, I offer
a garden view, a quiet room,
and a side of promised visits.

None of us can face dessert.
I pour more water,
lift a drink to my lips.

In silence you raise your glass,
in a toast, and across the table
blow a kiss at me.

Protection Racket

Dad slumps in the chair, staring at the floor
and, after we've eaten, my mother suggests
I entertain them both by playing the piano.
He bought it when they were newly-weds,
and she was cooking dinners on a rusty stove.
Legend has it they had to take the window out
to winch it into the first floor flat in Bayswater.

For fifty years, it's occupied the main room
of the family home, not been tuned for five.
The keys beneath unpractised fingers stick –
some fail to sound – but I pick out
the slow ripples of the Moonlight Sonata.

It's hardly Proust's Madeleine, but it strikes a chord
with the teenage girl who channelled angst
into Czerny exercises, and pages of Beethoven,
tense fingers tapping the slivers of ivory.
This is what they call a 'flow activity,' in which
you're supposed to lose yourself, but I find
too much is resonating.

You really enjoyed that, didn't you, dear?
my mother cajoles the unresponsive figure.
Yes, darling, very nice, he obediently monotones,
plucking with overgrown nails at elasticated trousers.
He seems to have a question to ask,
but sensing it will only show another dropped stitch
in the loosening fabric of his mind
she cuts him off with a platitude:
That was always a favourite, wasn't it?

We both know that for him, music ended with Baroque,
but she needs to stop this unravelling
and I recognise these lives are held together
with the duct-tape of pretence,
and that all he can offer is absence.

She worries later at the cost of his care package
but wants to be even-handed,
so I get back from work one day to find a cheque
and a jaunty note: *Here's your share of the dear old Bechstein*
that's gone to its new home.

Next time I visit, there are scars
beside the empty chair, where the piano legs had sunk
into the pile of the balding woollen carpet.

Tasting Session

You were the expert on this
and everything I attempted,
insisting that fine wine deserved the best treatment.
Polish the glasses, hold the decanter
up to the light as you trickle dark nectar into its belly.

Claret bottles, you instructed, have shoulders
to catch the sediment. Don't touch the dregs!
Swivel the glass, line it
with viscous swirls of wine;
get some air into it, so it can breathe.

The lead cuff round the bottle's neck reads:
Solum perfectum me attrahit.
I keep one, knead its yielding mass with my fingers.
I never managed the perfection you craved,
and, now infirmity defines your days,
no longer even aim at it.

My new hamartia is compassion,
sometimes misplaced or overdone,
but, like this wine, I've warmed from my cellared chill.
Empty rooms wear faint traces of an aftertaste;
the glass is half full. I'm flawed, but ready to be poured.

Ford Crossing

Some fords are easy to use,
with muddied ruts on either side;
or rough concrete slabs
beneath the peatbrown flow.
The water may move fast,
so no moss clings to mis-shapen stones.
Others we learn by season –
snow-melt boiling calls for diversion;
quiet summer smoothes flat ribbons
of water, from source to fall.

These last weeks I've watched
as you hesitated between
unknowing and the unknowable;
wished for your safe transit
across this unfamiliar ford.
I could not read the water levels,
nor offer a hand to steady you;
could only trust to decades
of bold stepping, your disregard
for wet feet, and desire to follow the path.

Today we carried an acorn bursting
with five leaves of accidental growth,
squirreled its tapering root
in the beechmast beside a stream;
placed a round stone, beautifully blemished,
to mark your passing and the oak tree's promise.
We forded the stream again,
climbed through the vale of consolation
and up into sunny moorland
where curlews cried your epitaph.

Oracle

For Suzanne Owen

Wood burns behind the glass door
of the stove, which creaks
as it releases heat into the room.
The year's about to pass;
whisky's poured, and the cloth is laid.
My friend lays cards, one Celtic being
for each Roman month, and another
for the whole year's fortune.

I tuck each aspiration into place:
unity, cunning, cleansing, resolution –
frog, wren, raven, hawk –
then out leaps Geàrr, depicted
silver-eared in moonlight,
poised between worlds
I thought to keep in place,
shape-shifter inviting surrender.

They say this creature of the Goddess
will show me how to negotiate
times of change; balance
channelled messages from elsewhere
with the clamour of the here and now.
I linger round liminalities, petition
for intuition; raise a glass
to harvest, rebirth, sacred fire.
The chimes begin.

Spa Break

A figure-skater in soft slippers,
she sketches shapes on my spine,
her work marked by the tracery she leaves.
Warmed fingers find knots,
pop them like bubblewrap;
she poises a fingertip on the summit
of my shoulder blade. Her tunic rustles
as she reaches for more oil,
then both thumbs glide in a long crossed chassé
to the edge of the towel,
and, because she is a stranger to me,
my body cannot anticipate the next twizzle,
or where her palm will come to rest,
nor how far she will venture to pummel
the contours stretched on her table.

Surfacing, my senses collect themselves,
as she cradles one forearm, shakes tension into limpness.
Now, knuckles knead the heel of my hand;
joints click in sympathy with the heating.
Wind and hail clatter, no-nonsense, against the windowpane.
She pivots, runs her hands from nape to coccyx,
skims a flattering hourglass on my back,
bends to whisper into my abandoned hair,
tells me she's done.

Map of Love

I'm off-grid; google maps has run out of juice.
The next charging point
is on a homeward bound train.
The setting sun, wedged between rooftops,
gives direction: instinct supplies the detail.
These are street names I remember
from narratives of the Great Fire;
places denoting plausible functions
when the city's hem dragged in surrounding fields.
Threadneedle Street, Leather Lane.
You can bypass the symbols of state
(Bank, Law Courts, Wren's domes and turrets
stranded amidst shiny tower blocks).

It's Friday night. Drinkers colonise the pavements,
washing off the week.
Their din spills into the dusk.
Solitary witnesses help more with route-finding.
A long walk, some warn,
but I was never afraid to put my best foot forward,
even though I lost my path at times,
sometimes got marooned for years.
Aspirational destinations seemed so right
at the time. The terminus is closer now.
Screeches of braking rolling stock echo
in the cutting by Farringdon Way.
To know where I'm heading next
I need to read your messages,
which pinged into my phone
as the battery raced into the red.

Seated, I click the charger into the socket.
Life surges into the screen in my palm.
The train lurches out of the station.

Aphasia

The poet has nothing left in his mouth
but kisses.
She has borrowed his words;
offers them back with no comment.
He collects them, one at a time,
when he gets round to it;
translates them with the touch
of a fingertip; misreads
the message she spells out
in candy love-hearts, spilled
onto the sheets; crunches
their sacramental speech
onto greedy tongues.
They share silence.

Notes

Page 9: The final lines of *Fall* refer to Jane Goodall's definition of man as 'a tool-making creature.'

Page 16: The 'found' element in *First Climb* was an item about honey collecting on the Radio 4 Food programme 29 September, 2015.

Page 19: The title of *Lost in the Wood* comes from 'Someone to Watch Over Me,' Ira Gershwin, 1926.

Page 24: The definitions given in *Definitions of a Shipwreck* of different types of wreckage have particular status in maritime law.

Page 40: In *A 64, es ist vollbracht* ('it is finished') comes from J. S. Bach Cantata BWV82, *Ich Habe Genug*.

Page 42: The word 'discalced' refers to those members of a religious order who go barefoot.

Page 46: In *Tasting Session, Solum perfectum me attrahit* translates as 'only perfection attracts me' and *hamartia,* the Greek word translated as 'sin', literally means 'aiming at but missing the mark'.

Page 50: *Map of Love* shares its title with a novel by Ahdaf Soueif.

Indigo Dreams Publishing Ltd
24, Forest Houses
Cookworthy Moor
Halwill
Beaworthy
Devon
EX21 5UU
www.indigodreams.co.uk